The Sales Value Chain:
A Guide to Creating Value for Your Customers & Your Career

By Dave Krentzman

The Sales Value Chain:
A Guide to Creating Value for Your Customers & Your Career
Published by SalesMentor.Net Publishing

Copyright © 2020 David A. Krentzman
All rights reserved

No part of this book may be reproduced or transmitted in any form or by any means electronically or mechanically, including photocopying, recording by any information storage retrieval system without permission in writing from the author.

Cover design by A.L. Sirois
Edited by Grace Marcus
Photograph courtesy of the author

Dedication

Being in sales for over forty years selling electronics, computer equipment, consulting services, sales training, professional services, health products, and audio equipment, taught me a great deal about my chosen profession. I've faced challenges and mistakes, successes and failures, and learned to enjoy my career with all of its ups and downs.

While still in high school and working as a part-time sales assistant in a department store selling 45s, LPs, posters, and record players, I first discovered the fun, excitement, and satisfaction that could be gained by being of service through selling.

My immediate supervisor was Sally White. Sally was in her late 30s, vivacious, warm, with a wonderful laugh, and playful nature. She also enjoyed a friendly relationship with many of her customers. Sally was highly knowledgeable regarding musicians and music, especially jazz, and her recommendations were welcomed by our clientele. Sally made working and selling fun. Her lively banter, her ability to satisfy customer's interests in music, and the pleasure she gained from helping others were contagious, inspiring, and amazing.

Sally's lessons of putting customers first, developing strong relationships, providing value through specialized knowledge, and being of service to others made a deep impression on me. It has been the foundation upon which I built my sales career.

This book is dedicated to Sally White. Without her, I may never have found the calling that changed my life.

Dave Krentzman –November 2020

Introduction

This is not a sales training book.
There are plenty of those.

It is not about a rigid sales methodology however effective it may be.
This is a guide to incorporating the sales training and strategies you have already received to make selling more productive, effective, and lucrative.

This material is meant to enhance, not replace, sales instruction.
Use it to sharpen your understanding of concepts proven to bring positive results.

The following pages offer tips, insights and strategies to help you sell better and improve your success rate. My insights have been developed over a 40-year career that has brought me into contact with various sales trainings and methodologies, and great mentors. I realized early on that any particular selling strategy was subjective and therefore worked best for salespeople whose personality, habits, and style most closely aligned to its originator. From each of these sources, I took the pieces and portions I felt were most relevant and meaningful to me. My suggestion is for you to do the same with the content you are about to experience. Take away the nuggets that are most meaningful and make them your own.

Table of Contents

Chapter 1 – Sales is an Honorable Profession   1

Chapter 2 - The Sales Value Chain   3

Chapter 3 - Create Value-Driven Relationships   8

Chapter 4 - Develop Specialized Knowledge   11

Chapter 5 – Be Yourself to Develop Your Selling Style   13

Chapter 6 - You Can't Build a Reputation on What You are Going to Do   17

Chapter 7 - Goals and Goal Setting   19

Chapter 8 - Selling is the Transfer of Value   22

Chapter 9 - Sellin' Ain't Tellin'   25

Chapter 10 - Understanding Sales Tension   30

Chapter 11 – B.U.D. – The 3-Legged Stool of Selling   34

Chapter 12 – Proactive Selling   38

Chapter 13 – Build Strong Relationships   42

Chapter 14 – Earning Trust and Credibility   44

Chapter 15 - Work for Others, While You Run Your Own Business   46

Chapter 16 - Leverage Your Contacts   50

Chapter 17 – Make Cold Calling More Effective   54

Chapter 18 – To Develop Big Deals, Start Small   57

Chapter 19 - Prepare for Success   61

Chapter 20 – Guide Your Prospects   63

Chapter 21 - Become an Effective Facilitator   65

Chapter 22 - Don't Leave Money on the Table   68

Chapter 23 – Maximize Your Compensation Plan   71

Chapter 24 - Put It All Together   74

Chapter 25 – Focus on the Input, Not the Outcome   76

Chapter 26 – Enjoy the Journey   78

Chapter 1 – Sales is an Honorable Profession

Sales is an honorable profession. The majority of people appreciate the benefits of what is being sold to them, especially when they have a good buying experience. Many times, customers are unaware of solutions that products and services can provide. Consequently, they are very grateful for the insight, creativity, and knowledge salespeople bring to their interaction.

So why, when you tell some people that you sell for a living, do they shrink from further conversation?

There will always be charlatans in any walk of life, sales included. The mental picture of the glad-handing, fast-talking, and unscrupulous used car salesman or carnival barker is still foremost in the mind of many people when they think about salespeople. Others only picture salespeople as duping customers into buying things they neither need or can afford. Movies and books have perpetuated this image, and no doubt there have been plenty of circumstances where this has been true. Unfortunately, the majority of hard-working and ethical sellers have been painted with this broad brush of dishonest activities.

Let's set the record straight about the realities of the sales profession.
To enjoy a successful career in sales requires honesty, integrity, hard work and a dedication to serving others. Your ultimate success will be determined by how effectively you incorporate these behaviors in your work.

Dave Krentzman

TO ENJOY A SUCCESSFUL CAREER IN SALES REQUIRES HONESTY, INTEGRITY, HARD WORK AND A DEDICATION TO SERVING OTHERS.

Salespeople play an important role in our economy. We facilitate the movement of goods and services between those who provide them and those who benefit from them. We offer information, guidance, and perspective to customers. We bring competition to the marketplace, which helps drive prices down and service up. Salespeople keep employed all manner of businesses, their staff and workers, shippers and handlers, and all associated people along the value and supply chains. Salespeople are essential to our way of life.

And yet, interestingly, the job salespeople do is not as well thought of or admired as the engineers, scientists, researchers, designers, and other professionals that salespeople directly or indirectly keep employed. This is possibly because of the low barrier to entry into the profession. You don't need a degree of any sort. You don't need specialized knowledge to start. You don't even need to know anything about selling. What you do need is a desire to better yourself, acquire life-long skills, improve your economic situation, be of service, and enjoy interacting with others. And, while there are endless products and services to sell, the key to success is your ability to transfer their intrinsic and practical value to buyers.

Chapter 2 - The Sales Value Chain

At the core of a buying transaction is the value a salesperson needs to convey from the first interaction with a buyer to the final steps in the buying process. The value a product or service provides, the communication skills, product knowledge, urgency and reliability that the salesperson demonstrates, are all links in establishing and creating value. Creating value for prospects and customers through sales activities is a significant differentiator that will lead you to outpace your peers and competitors. Value is both tangible and intangible. The tangible is how well the product or service solves a buyer's needs. The intangible is the belief a salesperson instills in a prospect that doing business with them and their company will produce a positive outcome.

> *CREATING VALUE FOR PROSPECTS AND CUSTOMERS THROUGH SALES ACTIVITIES IS A SIGNIFICANT DIFFERENTIATOR THAT WILL LEAD YOU TO OUTPACE YOUR PEERS AND COMPETITORS.*

There is a continuum in the value that salespeople provide to their customers. These salespeople understand that building a relationship with their customers, whether for the short or long-term, is essential to their success. They interact with their clients in more than just an order-taking capacity. They predicate their relationships on giving good service in all of their interactions and offer educated guidance, consistent follow-through on promised actions and customer requests, and integrity in their commitments and business dealings. This behavior builds trust and respect between the customer and the salesperson. Over time, trust and respect manifest in a relationship where the salesperson becomes what's known in sales jargon as a trusted advisor. This is the highest level of sales relationship and at this level, there is very little selling in the traditional sense. The salesperson now becomes part of the customer's team to help design, budget, or execute projects. It allows a salesperson to ask favors such as pushing through paperwork or brokering a special meeting and have it well received by the customer.

The Power of a Trusted Advisor

ALL SALESPEOPLE START THEIR JOURNEY ON THE CONTINUUM TO TRUSTED ADVISORS AS SIMPLY A VENDOR IN THE MINDS OF THEIR PROSPECTS.

The power of a trusted advisor can be illustrated by the example of a life-sciences company that had a mission-critical project that involved cyber-security testing of a hand-held device. The device was designed to communicate with a medication dispensing appliance worn by a patient. Critical health information from the appliance was monitored by the device and then transmitted via Bluetooth. This information was then uploaded to the Cloud and from there to the appliance manufacturer. In order to bring the new device to market, the company needed FDA approval of the cyber-security of the patient's information.

The project had multiple workstreams. As a result of the excellent work by the technical consultants and the relationships built at multiple levels of management, my company was awarded the entire project. Our team had as many as nine discrete workstreams underway over the year we spent working with the customer. My technical colleagues became an integral part of the customer's project team. They sought our advice and counsel, shared budgets, and quickly granted approvals. Collaboration was the working model. Ultimately, the FDA approved the device. This had a significant impact on the customer's sales and stock price. This piece of business would never have happened had it not been for the trusted relationships that had been established.

All salespeople start their journey on the continuum to trusted advisors as simply a vendor in the minds of their prospects. Many products and services are perceived by customers as a commodity with little information to differentiate one from another. To buyers, what matters most is identifying the right solution to their needs, competitive cost, timely availability, and functional quality. For salespeople, the challenge is to differentiate themselves and their company's products and services from the commodity mindset of customers and establish some basis for a continuing relationship. This is most often done through efficient service, product knowledge, prompt issue resolution, and courtesy. A salesperson needs to give a customer a reason to think of them the next time they need a similar or related product and establish enough rapport and credibility so that they can solicit additional business and the customer will be willing to take their call.

Experience has shown that it isn't possible in all salesperson/customer relationships to develop a trusted advisor status. Engendering mutual trust and respect often takes many interactions over an extended period of time to impress upon a customer the salesperson's ability to deliver value and the manner in which they go about their business. A customer may only purchase some products once or infrequently. This gives a salesperson limited exposure to prove their worth. There are, however, certain characteristics that a salesperson can display no matter how few and far between their dealings with a customer may be. These characteristics make a distinct impression upon a buyer and establish the basis upon which a trusted advisor status may develop. The trusted advisor is:

- **Motivated by service**
- **An effective communicator**
- **A problem solver**
- **A relationship builder**

- **Low pressure**
- **Non-confrontational**

A salesperson should always be striving to deliver value and keep the customer's needs and benefits utmost in their mind and actions. Trusted advisor status is a highly prized level of relationship that may last for years to the mutual benefit of all.

SUCCESSFUL SELLING BEGINS WHEN PREPARATION MEETS OPPORTUNITY.

As every journey of a thousand miles starts with a single step, so too does your journey to trusted advisor status begin with an initial contact. Ask yourself these questions:

- **How are you positioning what you sell, the company you represent, and your role in the sales process?**
- **Are you creating an upbeat, positive interaction?**
- **Are you focused on providing the best, most responsive service possible?**
- **Have you established enough rapport to close the sale if that is appropriate, or to earn the next step in your sales process if that is what is needed?**

Successful selling begins when preparation meets opportunity. And since a sales opportunity flows from your first interaction with a prospect, you will quickly know if you are prepared to sell or not. This means that the value you bring to your customers is based on more than how personable or helpful you are. While most often it is not necessary for you to be a product or service expert, it is always important to be conversant enough with what you are selling to hold an intelligent conversation. At whatever level you are engaged in the sale, the knowledge you have about your products and services is key to building your value as part of the sales process.

Whether you become engaged in a sales opportunity through an inbound or outbound lead, a website request for information, a chance meeting at a networking function, or the myriad of ways you may meet prospects, each interaction is yours to move along to whatever level of success you can accomplish. The sales value chain is a continuum with each new prospect and customer to whom you sell. Keep the continuum in mind as you do your job and it will provide the perspective you need to stay fresh and focused along the journey of your sales career.

Chapter 3 - Create Value-Driven Relationships

Delivering value is the basis on which successful selling and long-term business relationships are created and sustained. Buyers want more than features and benefits from what they purchase. They want to receive real value from what they buy. Value is perceived in many different ways and is almost always seen as getting what is paid for and then some.

Representing products and services that deliver value is key to creating value-driven business relationships. Look at what you sell:

- **Does it deliver on the promises made in your marketing materials?**
- **Is the feedback from your buyers positive or negative?**
- **Do you believe in its worth?**
- **Are you proud to sell it?**

It is important that you answer yes to these questions. If not, find something else to represent. If what you sell can't be sold with confidence and belief in its merits, you will be setting yourself up for either failure or frustration. Repeat business is the lifeblood of any business enterprise. If you disappoint your customers they won't be back for another purchase. If you satisfy, and even better delight them, repeat business and referrals to new buyers will most likely be in your future.

UNDER PROMISE AND OVER-DELIVER.

There is a phrase you may hear as relates to the products and services you sell: Under promise and over-deliver. A salesperson should strive to represent what they sell as accurately as possible without setting unrealistic expectations as to the results that a customer can expect. The buyer can then have an opportunity to experience performance from their purchase that may exceed expectations. Giving a realistic picture of what your products and services can do in relation to what the customer needs them to do, will also help you sleep at night. Returns and project issues are a normal part of doing business. Overselling, or selling a solution that you know isn't a good fit for a customer will always end poorly. Once this happens it is almost impossible to regain your customer's trust and business.

Value-driven relationships have to be built on trust; there is no exception. A decision to buy from you needs to be justified and rewarded. Remember, your customer's job may be on the line if what they buy creates a bigger problem than the one they are trying to fix.

You can also show value by referring your prospects to another product or service that will better serve their needs. This means that you go beyond simply telling a prospect what you sell won't be a good solution if you know a better way for them to solve their problem. When you display candor and honesty it creates a favorable impression and a refreshing experience for skeptical buyers.

> *YOUR BUSINESS DEALINGS SHOULD ALWAYS BE LEGAL, MORAL, AND ETHICAL.*

Value-driven relationships work because both the buyer and seller have a stake in each other's success. The seller benefits through earned commissions and job security, the buyer benefits by satisfying their need or solving their problem. This sets up a win-win scenario. As long as each benefit, the relationship will continue.

It is true that not all sales relationships are driven by value. Some salespeople see winning business at any cost as their goal. They see the dollars that can be earned by closing business and are willing to use any tactic whether or not it is ethical or legal. This is selling based on personal gain and focused solely on how they may profit. While it is possible to win business in this manner, it is not sustainable without constantly needing to find new customers. Buyers quickly recognize that they are not receiving value from their salesperson and move on. Long-term, valuable relationships become very difficult to cultivate and retain.

Your business dealings should always be legal, moral, and ethical. These qualities will inform how and what you choose to sell. This allows the freedom to build value-driven relationships because you know that you will always try to do the right thing for your customers.

Build your business relationships on these principles, strive to provide value in every interaction and you will have the foundation for a successful sales career.

Chapter 4 - Develop Specialized Knowledge

How would your success rate improve if you focused on developing specialized knowledge about your product line?

Is there a specific product or service that would make you the most money and in which you have the most interest?

If you become the sales expert in a particular area would it open up new opportunities for you?

THERE ARE MANY WAYS TO GAIN SPECIALIZED KNOWLEDGE. MOST ARE FREE OR OF MINIMAL COST.

Becoming an expert can advance your career. It will enable you to not only hold your own in a conversation with a prospect or customer but to also advance the sales process by providing relevant information that may generate new or additional business. Your prospects and customers usually strive to stay current with their industry and the products and services they buy. If you can contribute to their knowledge, your value to them will increase. You and your company's name will be at the top of their list when there is a need that falls within the products and services you sell.

There are many ways to gain specialized knowledge. Most are free or of minimal cost. You can find product trainings online for virtually anything you sell. The trainings are often in the form of a pre-recorded tutorial or training session given by a product expert from the manufacturer. Sellers can attend live, or archived, webinars that are designed to inform and educate sellers in the technical and functional value of the products and services they represent. Your employer may offer Lunch 'n Learn sessions that feature an expert from your company who will explain and demonstrate key information about what you sell. There are usually many articles to read online that offer explanatory information. And, there are a wide range of online industry-specific web sites. Most of these are free and only ask that you sign up to view the content they provide. Take advantage of as many of these opportunities as you can.

Another excellent way to obtain specialized knowledge is to talk with your prospects and customers. Potential customers can teach you a great deal through your conversations. Never be shy about asking them questions when it appears they have information that will further your knowledge. If you sell with technical partners, listen intently during customer meetings and conference calls when they present information and field customer questions. Their product knowledge and practical experience can be invaluable. Ask questions of your technical partners and develop a good working relationship with them. Your technical peers will almost always be very willing to share what they know. The more information you have about the products and services you sell, the better.

As you gain specialized knowledge about your industry, products, services, and trends, you become more valuable to prospects, customers, and your sales organization. This is an effective way to separate yourself from other salespeople in your industry and make a lasting impression to your clients. By sharing information your customers may need to make informed decisions, you offer them value. And, you will be recognized as a prepared and informed salesperson, just the type of person from whom your prospects and customers will want to buy.

If it sounds like I'm suggesting you go back to school to become an expert about what you sell, you're right. Become a student of your industry and strive to constantly learn more about what you sell, its uses, and the value it can bring to specific customers and circumstances. Take time to learn and keep learning throughout your career. You will become known for your expertise and it can lead to higher earnings and unexpected career opportunities.

Chapter 5 – Be Yourself to Develop Your Selling Style

Choosing the way in which you sell is like deciding on the flavor of ice cream that best suits your tastes and appetite. You may choose to be hard-driving in your prospecting, qualifying, and closing, or you may prefer a more temperate approach that puts less pressure on you, your prospects, and customers. You can follow the many selling systems, approaches, and processes that are well documented and taught by a wide range of individuals, consultants, and classroom instructors. Your employer may have chosen a sales methodology and require you to follow it. Or, you may have learned your sales skills through trial and error without any formal training. Just like ice cream, there are sometimes too many choices, making it hard to decide which will best satisfy and fit you.

An individual's selling style and philosophy are greatly influenced by their personality, the products and services they sell, the pay plan, sales training, and the environment in which they sell. Regardless of the sales method or philosophy one follows, certain personal attributes contribute to a salesperson's success. These attributes are:

- **Integrity, honesty, reliability**
- **Empathy, courtesy, generosity**
- **Personal grooming, table manners**
- **Speech habits, writing skills, creative thinking**

This list is meant to convey some of the qualities that, if developed, aid in successful selling. The idea is to remove whatever obstacles under your control that may turn a positive impression of you into a negative one. People do business with people they like, and cultivating these attributes reduces the chance of turning off a prospect or customer, thereby jeopardizing a deal.

Talking politics or religion has no place in the sales process. If you want to be social with your customers and prospects outside of doing business, be forewarned that friendliness, not friendship, is usually more appropriate. You take a big risk when you assume that a relationship alone will win business. It can often help you gain access to a decision maker. However, this person will always follow their own agenda that may differ sharply from yours. Doing business with a friend has cost many friendships. Be friendly, develop your relationships. But be careful not to confuse friendliness with friendship.

Use entertainment events and dinners to build relationships with prospects and customers. A cardinal rule for these occasions, especially events such as golf or a ballgame, is to never talk business unless the guest brings it up first. The goal is to build a more personal relationship than one that is solely focused on extracting business. Rewarding a good customer with a special event is a great way to show appreciation for the work that has been awarded. Using this approach may be helpful in gaining further access to conversations and meetings. It never assures, and it should never be assumed, that entertainment is a direct link to closing business. Become aware of which of your customers and prospects accept invitations solely to take advantage of your generosity and then take them off your future invite list.

Selling has a number of Golden Rules:

- **Be of service to others and financial, career, and reputational rewards will follow**
- **Develop specialized knowledge so that you become more valuable to your customers and employer**
- **Find a mentor with whom you can be completely honest regarding your difficulties and challenges, and who can guide you towards improvement**

- **Infuse your selling with your personality and don't try to imitate others, which will allow you to develop the skills needed to be successful and show a genuine face to colleagues and those with whom you do business**

TO BE TRULY EFFECTIVE IN SELLING, IT IS CRITICAL TO USE YOUR PERSONALITY AND NOT EMULATE ANYONE, EVEN THOSE SALESPEOPLE WHO YOU PERCEIVE AS THE MOST SUCCESSFUL.

Remember that you can't and shouldn't sell to everyone. Some prospects and customers will be too difficult to work with either because of a personality mismatch or that they are exceedingly unpleasant, mean, calculating or dishonest. It is not always your choice whether to deal with these people. Stay grounded in your integrity, sales philosophy, and commitment to your career. Never sacrifice your future for the short-term gain of a sale based on improper discounting or other questionable business practices. It will almost always come back to haunt you later.

To be truly effective in selling, it is critical to use your personality and not emulate anyone, even those salespeople who you perceive as the most successful. This is not to say that observing coworkers, trainers, and more experienced salespeople isn't helpful. It is. The point is that these people are successful in part because they have internalized their experiences, developed their methods, and learned to express themselves genuinely.

A big part of selling is your ability to gain the trust and confidence of your prospects and customers through your words and actions when they feel you are being truthful in your conversations and responses. Your willingness to express humor, candor, and sincerity that reflect your true feelings, provides a customer the opportunity to get to know you as an individual, not just a salesperson intent on making a sale.

A successful salesperson acts as a facilitator, translator, and guide. It is these roles that make the profession of selling so important and potentially lucrative. It is true that some people make a great deal of money selling illegal, unwholesome, and unhealthy products and services. However, this should be perceived as rendering a disservice to their buyers. It is best to provide products and services that make the world a better place. There is a wide opportunity in the marketplace for sellers. A good rule of thumb is to make sure that what you sell and the company whose products you represent are legal, moral, and ethical. This way you will sleep better at night and get to enjoy your relationships, efforts and financial rewards.

It can take many years to fully develop a selling style. It will take time for you to develop yours. Remember that successful selling is more than just closing a sale. It is establishing and maintaining productive relationships and taking personal responsibility for following through on commitments to customers and colleagues. Develop a positive sales philosophy that shows you at your best and it will guide you through the ups and downs of your career

Chapter 6 - You Can't Build a Reputation on What You are Going to Do

Your success as a sales professional isn't assured. When you start out, no one is going to hire you into a senior position, give you the best territories and accounts, or pay you commissions based on what you are going to accomplish. You will be hired because someone sees something in your background, education, drive, and personality that encourages them to believe you have the makings of a successful salesperson. Usually, you will be given some level of sales training and an introduction to your new employer's products and services. Then you will be assigned a quota, a list of prospects to contact, a desk and phone, and your manager's best wishes for success.

Selling, by its very nature, is a learned profession and craft. You can read countless books, take an endless number of sales methodology courses, and attend webinars covering how to sell virtually any type of product or service. However, it is not until you try to put these theories into practice that you learn to sell. This is also when you find out if a career in sales is something that you truly want and are willing to do the hard work needed to excel. As many would-be salespeople find out, it's not for everyone.

Creating a successful track record in sales takes time, patience, persistence, and losing more often than winning. Selling is a highly experiential learning environment. The doing is the most effective way to hone and then sharpen the attitude and many skills that enables a seller to reach, communicate with, and sell to individuals that they have never met.

You will build your reputation as you continue to learn and grow. Success doesn't happen overnight, and if you keep this in mind it will serve you well. There is plenty of excitement and reward in the sales profession. There is also a significant amount of frustration, grunt work, and disappointment. Your attitude and persistence are as much a part of the reputation you are building, as are the sales you close and the quotas that you achieve. Building your reputation so that former colleagues will remember you long after you stop working together is key. You never know when one of them may come calling and ask you to join them in an exciting new opportunity. At this point, your reputation will precede you and the sum total of your sales journey will set you up for a senior position, the best territories, and accounts, and the opportunity to make more commissions than you thought possible.

CREATING A SUCCESSFUL TRACK RECORD IN SALES TAKES TIME, PATIENCE, PERSISTENCE, AND LOSING MORE OFTEN THAN WINNING.

How you treat your co-workers is equally important to your future, as are the sales you close and the customers with whom you do business. Strive to become the salesperson that everyone in your company wants to work with. Recognize early on that interpersonal relationships are extraordinarily important to your success and reputation. If you inspire others to do their best for you and your customers, everyone wins. If you don't, it is usually you that suffers. Treat your co-workers with respect, uphold your responsibilities, communicate well, and give praise and recognition for their contributions in a public way. Your ability to be seen as a leader who creates success, and not as someone who simply takes credit for the work of others, is remembered and appreciated and is central to building the kind of reputation that you want to enjoy and for which you are known. It's important to keep in mind that a good reputation is the hardest thing to earn and the easiest thing to lose.

Chapter 7 - Goals and Goal Setting

As a professional salesperson you have ambition to accomplish certain goals. You may want to earn a specific amount of money, advance to a more senior role, move into management or simply pick up experience, expertise, and skills that will enable you to become more valuable to future employers. Regardless of the motivation, it is very important that you clearly envision and articulate what you are trying to accomplish by establishing goals that are as well-defined as possible. This will help you create value for yourself at the same time as you work to create value for your employer and your customers.

Your manager will give you achievement goals. They may be in the form of a quota, the desired number of new customers, gross or net margin targets, or a range of other performance measurements. These are external goals that are necessary to accomplish, however they are not as motivating as internal goals. Internal goals are generated by what you want to achieve and the resulting benefits that will accrue to you.

> *THE MOST EFFECTIVE GOAL SETTING IS WHEN YOU ALIGN PERSONAL GOALS WITH THE DEMANDS OF YOUR JOB.*

Working strictly to make a certain amount of money is ineffective as a motivator. Money is an abstract concept and cannot create a strong emotional pull. You can use the goal of reaching a certain income as a motivator if it relates to what that income will enable. It might buy a new home or a vacation that you could otherwise not afford. It might give you the ability to purchase certain items that are currently out of reach. It might allow you to plan effectively for retirement. Only you will know what is personally most important. The clearer you can make your desired outcomes, the stronger will be the emotional pull and motivators.

The most effective goal setting is when you align personal goals with the demands of your job. If you are able to see how accomplishing one enables the other, great. If not, you may want to either realign your personal goals or find a new position. Goals should be set on what you believe can be achieved in your current position. Realistic goals keep you from getting discouraged and giving up. Monitor regularly your progress towards your goals so that you can course correct, if necessary, and pat yourself on the back when appropriate.

Stretch goals can also be useful. These are goals that are beyond what you believe you can accomplish, but within the realm of possibility. Stretch goals need special effort to realistically accomplish, so make sure you align them with extra special rewards. Keep personal goals to yourself, or only share with others who you can trust will not judge if you fall short. You want your internal motivation to pull you forward, not set you up for discouragement.

The external goals given by your manager are often reviewed weekly during a sales team meeting or one-on-one. Motivation to stay on track with these goals is usually provided by wanting to compare favorably with your sales peers, stay in the good graces of your manager, and ultimately, stay employed. Find time each week to review your internal goals because accomplishing your personal goals will have a direct, positive effect on exceeding your manager's goals. It is also a good idea to create milestones on the way to fully accomplishing each goal so that you can see the progress or lack of progress, you are making. This will help to keep you on track.

The way to set effective internal goals is to:

- **Decide on your goals**
- **Envision what accomplishing your goals will enable you to have, do, or become**
- **Write down your goals and keep them to yourself**
- **Be clear and realistic in what it will take to achieve them**
- **Conceive a plan of action and get started**
- **Keep track of progress towards your goals**
- **Make adjustments in your actions as needed**
- **Reward yourself for accomplishments**

Goal setting is fundamental to achievement. As the old saying goes, "If you don't know where you are going, you usually end up someplace else." Know where you are heading so that you can be rewarded for the hard work it will take to get there. This is the act of creating value for yourself and will manifest additionally in increased self-esteem, self-worth, confidence, and belief in your future. Once you realize that it is possible to set and achieve goals, you will use this process to envision and accomplish more and more exciting possibilities. It is a technique that never gets old and can be used for your entire career.

Chapter 8 - Selling is the Transfer of Value

Selling is the transfer of value. Webster's Dictionary defines value as a fair return or equivalent in goods, services, or money for something exchanged; relative worth, utility, or importance. A fair return or equivalent in goods, services, or money for something exchanged; relative worth, utility.

Value can be transferred from one person to another, one business to another, or any situation in which a service, product, concept, or intangible is offered for sale. Value manifests in the benefits that products and services bring to customers and clients. Value can take many forms and can be measured by the extent it solves or satisfies the purchaser's needs or desires.

- **Have you taken the time to understand the value of what you sell?**
- **Do you know enough about the market for your products and services?**
- **Do you know where what you have to offer is most needed?**

These are critical questions to answer and to keep revisiting. The more you envision where what you sell can be of the greatest value, the more opportunities will present themselves. When prospecting, you will have a range of options to suggest as potential areas of interest. Opportunities will also open up during conversations with your current customers when discussing their existing and anticipated needs as you suggest additional uses for your offerings. Selling and delivering value, not the specific products or services you offer, is what will attract prospects and keep customers.

Your job as a salesperson is to facilitate the transfer of value through the sales process. There are many ways you can start the transfer of value. Email, texts, phone calls, online meetings, in-person meetings, webinars, speaking engagements, and all manner of marketing vehicles provide the platforms to get your message out to prospects and customers. The better the message aligns with your products and services proven value, and your ability to deliver the message, the more effective the outcome. Never overpromise or misrepresent what you sell. If you schedule a meeting or call based on false or misleading information it almost always annoys the prospect and becomes a dead-end for future opportunities.

SELLING AND DELIVERING VALUE, NOT THE SPECIFIC PRODUCTS OR SERVICES YOU OFFER, IS WHAT WILL ATTRACT PROSPECTS AND KEEP CUSTOMERS.

Take time to craft a value statement. This is a variation on the idea of an elevator pitch, a quick message you can deliver to a stranger. A simple message may be "I sell cars, or I'm a lawyer, or I'm a consultant." While this type of answer may seem straightforward, it doesn't say anything about the value you offer or the marketplace that you serve. The idea is to succinctly share information about the professional value you can provide.

A value statement must contain certain elements to be effective. These elements clearly express what your product or service does, the market it serves, and the value it provides. A well-crafted value statement can be used in all of the various ways of contacting a prospect. You simply tailor it to the vehicle you are using and the customer you are contacting.

YOUR ABILITY TO EASILY ARTICULATE YOUR VALUE STATEMENT IS CRITICAL TO YOUR SUCCESS.

As you develop your value statement think about your target market and the fundamental problems that you solve for your customers. Go beyond the obvious and distill the features and benefits of your products and services to get at the essence of their value. If you are in the residential real estate business, instead of telling people that you sell real estate, your value statement could sound like this: "My name is John Green. I help people buy their dream home and make the process easy and exciting." If you are a management consultant, instead of simply saying you are a consultant, it might sound like this: "My name is Brenda Cauley. I work with corporate clients to solve complex business problems and improve their profitability." If you are a salesperson, instead of saying that you are in sales, your value statement might be: "My name is Paul Connor. I provide services to corporate clients and educational institutions to help manage their complex computing environments."

Your ability to easily articulate your value statement is critical to your success. Keep revising it until you are confident in its message and then practice it out loud to make it your own. Remember, you are not trying to tell a story, you are only trying to share the value your products and services offer in a way that furthers a conversation with your prospect. Sometimes you will just use the essence of your value statement, sometimes the whole message. The clarity you gain from creating and using a value statement will help you confidently interact with people you meet. It will turn up unexpected possibilities and opportunities for engagement.

Chapter 9 - Sellin' Ain't Tellin'

Expressing your products or services through a value statement is the first step in creating a dialogue that may lead to a sale. It is important to keep in mind that dialogues are two-sided; there needs to be a give and take between you and your prospect or customer.

While this is true, remember that the words coming from your customer or prospect are far more important than anything you have to say. Their words will often give you clues or significant guidance as to how your sales approach should continue or if it should be continued at all. Your prospect's buying needs and what it will take to make a deal, can only come from them. Without gaining a clear understanding, you won't be able to move the sales process along to a successful conclusion. Email and text correspondence have their place, however, they are poor substitutes for a live conversation.

You must share information, guidance, and perspectives with your prospects. Your customers want your opinions. However, their feedback contains key information upon which you can adjust your sales approach or decide to abandon your pursuit. Always stop talking immediately, even in mid-sentence, when prospects and customers start to talk. This is because what the customer has to say is infinitely more important than anything that you are saying. Take notes while they are talking. Afterward, if it is still appropriate, tell the prospect what it was you were about to say. Not only is this a more polite way to hold a conversation, it is just smart. Let the prospect lead while you listen and learn.

ALWAYS STOP TALKING IMMEDIATELY, EVEN IN MID-SENTENCE, WHEN PROSPECTS AND CUSTOMERS START TO TALK.

Listening is also of great value because when you show a prospect that you have heard what they have said, it's very flattering. Most people aren't used to others paying attention to them, especially a salesperson eager to get their point across. There will be many occasions when after a meeting with a prospect or customer in which they do 90% of the talking, you will be complimented about how great the conversation was. Of course, they did all of the talking! You will still be able to get across the points you need to convey and the prospect will most likely leave the appointment with a positive impression of you.

Listening without hearing is of little value. Don't pretend to listen, seeming to take in what is being said. Stay active in the conversation by interjecting questions or asking for clarifications. Selling is like a tennis match where prospect and salesperson volley through their dialogue. To be a good player you must respond to what is being said or asked with energy and thought. Stay in the game and your prospect will appreciate the attention and feel that you are truly invested in solving their problems.

Take notes when you are in conversation with your prospects and customers. You don't need to write down everything that is being said, however, notes will help you remember the important points without having to worry that you missed or have forgotten something. There is nothing worse than leaving a great meeting and trying to recall a specific comment, direction, or ask from the conversation. Taking notes also shows that you are interested in what is being said and is flattering to your prospect. To set up a more cordial and comfortable atmosphere for the conversation, ask if it is okay to take notes when your meeting starts.

A good example of the power of listening is from an experience a friend of mine had when trying to remodel his kitchen. What he wanted was to install new cabinets, counters, appliances, and a new floor. He planned to fix up his house and then sell it in a few years when he was ready to retire. A new kitchen was important, however, spending for a high-end, spare-no-expense kitchen was not part of his plan.

My friend called a kitchen remodeling outfit to come over and give him an estimate. He was a perfect prospect. Living in an upscale neighborhood in an expensive home, he had the financial resources to do whatever he wanted. Along with his wife, he was going to be involved in the planning and decision-making process for the new kitchen. He had a budget, a clear need, and both decision makers were going to be present during the conversation. There was only one problem. During the sales call, the salesman from the remodeling company forgot to listen.

"We told the salesman that we wanted a simple remodel with new counters, appliances, floor and cabinets," my friend explained. "We were pretty specific with our budget and gave him our goals for the project. He kept nodding and talking as if we were on the same page. But when the salesman presented his proposal it was for a kitchen that belonged in the Taj Mahal. It was nothing like what we had asked for. I even remember saying to him, didn't you hear a thing that we said? So, we got rid of him and called another kitchen contractor who actually listened to us. It was such a relief to know that the new guy would do what we wanted that we signed up with him right away."

IT'S CRITICAL THAT YOU LEARN TO BE AN EXCELLENT LISTENER BECAUSE YOUR PROSPECTS WILL ALWAYS GIVE YOU INFORMATION THAT CAN BE USED TO SOLVE THEIR PROBLEMS.

Listening is so important that it's hard to believe that the first salesperson could have missed the mark completely given all of the information and guidance that had been supplied by his prospects. He forgot the first rule of successful selling: ask questions to find out what your prospects want and how they want it. Then, if possible, give it to them just that way. And if appropriate, suggest helpful alternatives and options of which they may be unaware.

Too many salespeople hear only what they want to hear and make assumptions based on preconceived ideas about their prospects. In this case, it might have been assumed that since my friend and his wife lived in an expensive home, they would want only the best in a remodeling project. When the budget was shared, the salesman thought that the customer was low-balling and probably had a lot more money to spend. Even though their goals had been stated, the salesman figured that by adding certain pricey features and modifications the project could be expanded. And, he knew that expensive projects make for bigger commissions.

To be successful a salesperson must gain a clear understanding of what a prospect is trying to accomplish. It doesn't matter what type of product or service is being sold. The ability to recognize and comprehend a prospect's goals starts with the salesperson asking probing, fact-finding questions. It continues with the salesperson asking for clarification of anything that they have heard that may be open to misinterpretation. This process is known as active listening and it rewards both parties in the conversation with clear understanding and rapport.

The old saying: "The reason we were given two ears and one mouth was so that we would listen twice as much as we speak," is certainly relevant to quality selling. Remember, when a prospect or a client speaks, you must stop talking and listen. Your comments and insights can wait to be shared.

It's critical that you learn to be an excellent listener because your prospects will always give you information that can be used to solve their problems. What you sell, what you think, and what you know isn't important to your prospects until they believe that you are invested in taking care of their needs. Your goal must be to learn about what's in it for them. More than any words you can say, active listening demonstrates the level of concern and interest you have in their issues. Ultimately, people don't care how much you know until they know how much you care.

Chapter 10 - Understanding Sales Tension

If you have ever gone fishing and thrown a baited line in the water, you know that you want a fish to rise to the bait, bite on it and then feel the hook in its mouth as it tries to swim away. Suddenly, the line goes taut and you know the fish is hooked. All you have to do now is reel it in. This is the exciting part of fishing when there is action and your skill as a fisherman comes into play. You know that as long as there is tension on the line the fish is still engaged. Sometimes the fish wriggles free or the hook isn't set deep enough and suddenly the line goes slack and the fish is gone.

SALES TENSION IS AKIN TO FEELING A FISH ON YOUR LINE AND THE TAUTNESS OF STAYING ENGAGED UNTIL IT IS FINALLY CAUGHT.

We all know that prospects and customers aren't fish, however selling has fundamentals and dynamics that are similar to fishing. When working with a prospect or customer on a new sales opportunity, keep in mind the concept of sales tension. Sales tension is akin to feeling a fish on your line and the tautness of staying engaged until it is finally caught. Sales tension starts by finding out what your prospect wants and needs, and if it is within the capabilities of your products and services to deliver. Next, you present it in a form that entices engagement. If what you offer has sparked interest and you decide it is a viable opportunity, a next step should mutually be agreed upon. You can then start to judge the level of engagement, or sales tension, that the prospect is displaying. In fishing, if the line is taut or the line is slack, it helps you know if you have hooked the fish. Similarly, the tension in your sales interactions will help you understand where you stand in the sales process.

Sales tension indicators:

- **Open discussion of buying drivers**
- **Calls and emails are promptly returned**
- **Meetings are set and kept**
- **Postponed meetings are immediately rescheduled**
- **Next steps are agreed upon and fulfilled**
- **Proposals are requested**
- **Budgets are shared**
- **Appropriate decision makers are involved**
- **Timelines for purchases are discussed and agreed upon**
- **Paperwork such as vendor agreements and purchase orders are finalized**
- **Start or delivery dates are set**

Keep 'tugging the line' to ensure that the prospect continues to be engaged all through the sales process. Things can change quickly even in the most promising sales pursuit. It is better to cut bait and move on if the tension ceases or if it is clear the prospect is no longer on the line. This can be a hard decision to make, especially if you feel that you are losing the big one. No matter, there are many fish in the sea and it is important to spend your time in more productive fishing grounds.

Most sales come down to your ability to qualify a prospect all the way to a close. This may involve asking the hard questions from which salespeople often shy away. Hard questions can include asking for:

- **Candid feedback on a proposal**
- **Available budget**
- **Competitor's proposal**

- **Time-line for decision-making**
- **Approval process**

Most salespeople think of a closer as a hard-driving sales professional who doesn't take no for an answer and consistently finds ways to get to yes, right? Well, yes and no. Completing a sale with a signed purchase order is simply the culmination of a series of closes that start with the first interaction a salesperson has with a prospect. Closing is a process, not a single event.

The dictionary defines closing as bringing something to an end; final. In a sales process, this typically means getting a written approval or receiving a purchase order. In fact, there are multiple closes or decision points along the road to the completion of a buying transaction. Each requires a salesperson to use skill and training to guide the prospect to a positive conclusion. Each yes from your customer is a building block of the ultimate yes that you are pursuing.

One of the clearest ways to assess the viability of a sales pursuit is the continued willingness of a prospect to close on next steps. Rate your deals by the level of closed next steps and you will quickly understand where you should be spending your time and energy.

Finalizing a deal and getting an order should be a natural outcome from all of the closes that have taken place during a sales pursuit. This last step tends to get the most attention and generate the most excitement. Although it feels great to make a sale and experience a successful conclusion to all of your hard work, the final yes can seem almost anticlimactic. When you understand that the final yes is part of the continuum of yeses that have taken place, it will come as no surprise that closing is a process.

There are so many things outside of your control that can kill a deal, that it sometimes feels as if it takes a miracle for a sale to get done. If you remain aware of the level of your prospect's engagement through the whole sales cycle, it can keep you from wasting time and resources chasing a deal that will never close. Be realistic in your assessment of sales tension. It will save you frustration and stress, and give your prospect the freedom to stay or come back at a later date

Chapter 11 – B.U.D.
The 3-Legged Stool of Selling

There is real danger in not adequately evaluating whether a sales opportunity is worth pursuing. The following story illustrates this point:

The sales opportunity looked good. In fact, it looked so good that senior management was thrilled at the thought of landing the business. The prospective account was a major insurance company. The contact at the account was an Assistant Vice-President (AVP) who carried a lot of influence and assured the salesperson that he was the decision maker on the project.

Winning the account was not going to be easy. There was definitely competition. The Request for Proposal had gone out to ten vendors and there were three finalists in the running. While nothing was said out loud, the decision maker gave indications to the saleswoman that her organization was in the lead. Armed with encouragement from the AVP, the saleswoman and her senior management decided to put on a full-court-press to win the account.

> *MORE SALES ARE LOST, NOT AT THE END, BUT AT THE VERY BEGINNING OF A SALES PURSUIT.*

For the next fifteen months, they did everything they could to influence the decision and prove their worth. They attended endless meetings. Subject matter experts were flown in from great distances for high-level discussions with the prospective client. Consultants were put on-site at no charge to demonstrate their expertise. Even contractors were hired and paid to perform trial projects so that the prospect could see how well the seller was at staffing and project management.

The end result was that after fifteen months of hot pursuit and the expenditure of $100,000, the project was awarded to a competitor. It turned out that the Assistant Vice-President wasn't the real decision maker after all. The saleswoman and her senior management were selling to someone who couldn't buy.

Sound familiar? More sales are lost, not at the end, but at the very beginning of a sales pursuit. It is at the beginning of the sales process that strong qualifying skills are needed to determine a prospect's ability to do business. And not every prospect qualifies. That's right, not every sales opportunity is worth the time, effort, and resources that it will take to make a sale.

The BUD Rule

Qualifying a prospect is built on the BUD rule. There must be sufficient Budget available to spend on fixing an Urgent problem. There must be sufficient Urgency to the prospect's problems to warrant buying a fix. Finally, there must be someone who has the decision-making authority to spend the Budget to fix the Urgent problem. A potential sale cannot take place unless all three elements are in place.

Unfortunately, you can't always depend on your prospect to give a straight answer when asking about their Budget, Urgency, and Decision-making authority. The AVP in our story assured the saleswoman that he would decide who would win the project. The saleswoman believed him and the rest, as they say, is history.

So how can you know the truth? If you want to know how Urgent a certain problem is you must ask these questions:

- **How long has the company or individual had this problem?**

- **What have they tried to do to fix it up until now?**
- **What were the results?**
- **Why do they believe they weren't successful?**
- **What has been the financial cost of these problems?**

The answer to these questions will give you real insight into whether the problem is causing enough trouble to warrant a remedy. You can then ask:

- **Is there a Budget set aside to fix the Urgent problem?**
- **If not, can one be created?**
- **Which department or person controls the budget?**

You can ask your contact about the Decision process:

- **Where does the contact fit in the process?**
- **Who do they report to?**
- **Will they introduce you to that person?**
- **Will they set up a meeting for all of you?**

Be wary when you are told that your contact alone will make the decision and that you must deal only with them. That is a big red flag. Another red flag is if they will not give you the name of their boss or forbid you to contact that person. While it is true that in some situations a decision to purchase can be made by one person, it is almost always a decision-by-committee when significant dollars are going to be spent, or if the purchase will have a major impact on the buyer's organization.

Remember, it's better to walk away from a sale earlier than later if it doesn't qualify. There are so many elements that must come together to win business from a prospect. Many of these elements, such as a change in the business climate, a sudden acquisition or merger of the business, a change in decision makers or a redeployment of the intended budget are far beyond the salesperson's control. What is in your control starts with how well the prospect is qualified for Budget, Urgency, and Decision-making authority. Selling is truly a three-legged stool and no sale, project or engagement will take place unless all three elements are firmly in place.

Chapter 12 – Proactive Selling

The way to keep the initiative and drive things forward is to be proactive in all of your interactions. You are the one interrupting a prospect with a request for a conversation. Why would you expect someone who doesn't know you, or the reason why you are calling, to want to speak with you or return your call? You are responsible for initiating contact and it is up to you to make something happen. Far too many prospecting emails leave the return call up to the prospect. Instead of ending a prospecting voicemail or email telling the prospect to contact you, always tell them to expect a call within the next week. If they want to speak with you sooner, they can use the contact information you have provided.

This is an example of selling with urgency. Selling with an urgency to move things forward is a strategic differentiator in competing for business. Out-working, out-hustling, and out-thinking your competition places you in a position to respond to the speed at which business moves and buying decisions happen. When you follow up in a timely way it shows your prospects that you can be trusted to keep your word and commitments. Every interaction, where you do what you said you would do, reinforces and enhances the positive relationship you are building.

> **SELLING WITH AN URGENCY TO MOVE THINGS FORWARD IS A STRATEGIC DIFFERENTIATOR IN COMPETING FOR BUSINESS.**

Your prospects and customers often have urgency of their own in the decisions they make. If a project needs to be done in a certain timeframe, or a product needs to be purchased to fix a pressing problem, they need a salesperson that can match their level of urgency to get things done. The relationship you have built based on your responsiveness may be the deciding factor in whether or not you get their business.

There is a difference between selling with urgency and being overly aggressive when contacting and following up on calls, emails, and meetings. If you leave multiple voicemails or call your prospects and customers multiple times without leaving a message, your urgency can become annoying. Caller ID is now standard on most phones including corporate phone systems. If your number repeatedly flashes across the screen of people you're trying to reach, it creates a negative, not positive impression. People are busy with their work and returning your call or email may not have the priority you would like it to have.

Use a simple system to follow up on communications to your customers and prospects. First, let them know in your initial email or call that you will be in touch within a few days. Typically, wait three days to make your first follow up attempt. During the call, reference either the initial call or email to remind them who you are and why you are calling. If you don't connect directly, leave another voicemail. Then wait another four to five days to try again. At this point, if you cannot get your prospect or customer on the line, leave a final voicemail saying that you have tried to reach them a number of times, and not wanting to be a pest, will try them again in the future. Should they want to reach you, leave your phone number and email address and once again reference your initial call or email.

In many circumstances, it can take multiple calls or emails over weeks, months, or even a year to connect with certain prospects. During these times your voicemail and email messages should remain upbeat, positive, and courteous. Prospects know that you want to connect to sell them something. That's the nature of the relationship. Keep your interactions respectful and brief by not showing frustration or anger at their not being responsive. Selling with urgency is your urgency, not theirs. Be considerate and consistent. The industry in which you sell is full of prospects that move from one company and job to another. You just might have an opportunity to work with one of these difficult to reach prospects in the future. You want them to remember you in a positive way.

Proactive sellers:

- **Perform the right activities consistently and persistently until they see results**
- **Return phone calls and emails quickly, and get requested information, proposals, and other documents back to customers and prospects accurately and speedily**
- **Give great customer service and follow up even when it may be someone else's responsibility to do so**
- **Build relationships by doing what they say, to the best of their ability, without prompting and with a clear sense of purpose**

It is easy to get frustrated, discouraged, and run out of drive as a salesperson. There can be so many obstacles to making a sale, such as:

- **Prospects and customers don't make decisions fast enough**
- **The marketing department doesn't provide the leads, collateral, or presentations as quickly as you want them produced**
- **Potential sales are held up by decision makers going out-of-town, on vacation or out on sick leave**
- **The buyer with whom you have had a solid relationship changes jobs or companies, and the once-pending purchase order suddenly disappears**
- **Your best account is purchased by another company and the sales you just made or the services you are delivering are halted**

An effective technique to deal with these frustrations is to place a sticky note with a large 'P' for patience written on it to the front of your computer monitor. Why? To remind yourself daily that it takes time to get appointments and work through complete sales cycles. And while being patient for your business to develop, be as active as possible in calling, sending emails, working your network, and other activities to find more prospects. This is what it takes to succeed.

Proactive selling also means making that last call at the end of the day, or even after business hours, to the prospect you have been trying to reach for months. It means working over the weekend or even on vacation to finish the proposal that you promised by a certain date. It means having the understanding that business moves quickly and if you don't want to be left behind you have to act deliberately and with speed.

Remember, you can only control your actions and not those of your prospects and customers. And while it may seem that selling with a sense of urgency and patience are opposites, when it comes to selling, they are two sides of the same coin.

Chapter 13 – Build Strong Relationships

Selling is a person-to-person activity. Buying is different. Buyers have lots of choices when making a purchase. Social media, the Internet, and other electronic methods don't involve talking to a salesperson. Those buyers, who by choice or by necessity need to interact with a salesperson, often make buying decisions as a result of their experience with the salesperson. This is true whether the customer is speaking to an experienced sales pro, customer service representative, or inside salesperson.

Buyers want and expect you to have the knowledge and experience to guide them to the right product or service that matches their needs. This is a reasonable expectation. They also require a courteous and efficient interaction. If they find you responsive and motivated to make their buying experience enjoyable, so much the better. With many products and services competing to provide similar value, buyers often make their choice based on the experience they have had through the sales process.

People buy from people they like. The rapport they feel with you can be the deciding factor in their buying process. Your knowledge, experience, courtesy, and efficiency are important. If you personalize the buying experience and build rapport with a buyer, it can start a relationship that results in a single transaction or may last your entire career. Personalizing means investing the time, patience, good humor, and willingness to do the right thing for your customers. Give them the guidance toward better solutions than the ones they know about, tell them about discounts of which they may be unaware, and even suggest a competing product or service if you know yours isn't right for them. Telling a prospective buyer the truth rarely costs you anything. If you knowingly sell a customer the wrong item just to make a sale, it almost always comes back to bite you. Your integrity and ethical choices have far reaching consequences for your career.

PEOPLE BUY FROM PEOPLE THEY LIKE.

How you sell, the way you treat prospects and customers, and how you interact with your colleagues, all affect the way people perceive and work with you. You want and need to be the salesperson that everyone in your company wants to work with on their deals. You can't build a reputation on what you are going to do. Become the salesperson to whom your boss gives the best leads because he knows you will always do the right thing. Be the colleague that your delivery team wants on their projects because they appreciate how you treat them. Sell with integrity, honesty, good humor and responsiveness. It's actually easier to act in this manner than to come back later to fix all of the problems that result from doing expedient and questionable things. Experience has shown that always doing, or trying to do the right thing, is the best way to make career-long relationships with customers and colleagues. The hidden benefit is that you never know where these relationships may take you in the future.

Chapter 14 – Earning Trust and Credibility

Products and services such as insurance, consulting, and money management are what can be called intangibles or concepts. They don't have mass, color, size, smell, or feel. Selling these products and services requires that the salesperson engage the prospect's imagination, belief, confidence and trust that what is being purchased will solve their problems and offer benefits.

How is it possible to sell expensive products and services to a prospect who may have had no previous experience with the salesperson, their company, or offerings?

Selling concepts and intangible services are predicated on credibility, trust, and relationship. A prospect needs to buy the salesperson first, their company second, and the product or service third. Salespeople build credibility and relationship by establishing good rapport and taking a genuine interest in the prospect, their needs, and concerns. Generally, people do business with people they like. Rapport is a key element in helping to establish a positive relationship with a prospect to gain their trust that what is being offered is credible. Credibility is further enhanced by demonstrating knowledge of the prospect's particular industry or market segment.

A PROSPECT NEEDS TO BUY THE SALESPERSON FIRST, THEIR COMPANY SECOND, AND THE PRODUCT OR SERVICE THIRD.

Selling your company comes next. If you're selling for a well-known or established organization, it's easier to tout its merits. If you are selling for a company that is unknown to the prospect, it is critical that you provide positive evidence of its value. Marketing materials can help, although finding a thread of connection to the prospect's company is more persuasive. If you can reference an employee of the prospect's company that has had a positive experience with your service it will go a long way to build trust. Alternatively, if you can reference a customer in the same industry and share a brief case study, it creates a level of comfort for your prospect so they will feel assured that what you sell can be of real value.

Now that you have established rapport and your company's credibility, it's time to introduce your services. When selling an intangible such as insurance, consulting, professional, and financial services, it helps to use visual aids such as projections and deliverables scrubbed of customers' information. Real-life examples from previous engagements can also help the prospect clearly imagine the value you can provide. Industry awards and accolades and a list of representative customers will also support the positive message you are delivering.

Remember that when selling a concept or intangible, the prospect must have a significant amount of confidence in you, your company, and your services. Most importantly, first establish your own set of intangibles and concepts of caring, reliability and trustworthiness. This is the foundation that your prospect needs in order to confidently do business with you. Even though there may be many more steps to bring your deal to a close, you will have built your sales pursuit on the solid ground of credibility, trust, and relationship.

Chapter 15 - Work for Others, While You Run Your Own Business

Who you work for is not just the name of your employer, sales manager, or vice-president of sales. You were most likely hired by one of these people and they are the ones that assign your quota and performance goals. But do they earn your paycheck or commission? Are they concerned with supporting your family or paying for the new house you want to buy? Of course not. In the end, you work for yourself and your own rewards. Most salespeople think that they work for their boss. After all, if you don't satisfy the quota and metrics assigned to you, your job may be in jeopardy. Reviews of your work are critical to your advancement, potential raises, and standing in your sales organization.

There is a big difference in how you approach your job between doing what is required of you and pursuing larger goals. A competitive golfer wants to win against the competition while recognizing that their personal score is solely based on their individual performance. And so it should be in sales. While you can measure yourself against your peers, the real measure of success should be against the goals you set. By setting your own goals and striving to achieve them, you are essentially your own boss. Measure your performance against the level of success you decide to achieve.

THERE IS A BIG DIFFERENCE BETWEEN DOING WHAT IS REQUIRED OF YOU AND PURSUING LARGER GOALS.

There will always be obstacles that you must overcome even in the best working environments. How you face these obstacles and the actions you take to mitigate them will define your sales career. When you work for a company it is easy to come up with excuses why you may fall short of quota and the various metrics that measure your work output. Some of the excuses that you think may be stopping you are:

- **Marketing can't bring you any decent leads**
- **Delivery is late and sloppy**
- **Prospects and customers take forever to sign paperwork**
- **Management has unreasonable demands, and so on and so on**

While there may be circumstances outside of your control that weigh on your effectiveness, you also have your own decisions to make. Ask these questions:

- **Are these issues negatively impacting my personal business?**
- **What can I do to lessen their effect?**
- **Is there anything within my power that will move things forward and result in achieving my personal goals?**

When you leave solving the problems that block the success of your selling efforts to others, you will almost always be disappointed. It's your commission and your rank in the sales team that is on the line.

If you are looking for a name for your business try Me Incorporated. This is not to say that you should focus solely on what's in any particular selling situation that will benefit just you. Most selling is a collaboration between many groups, departments, or individuals in your company. People from these other areas have their personal and professional goals as well. Your ability to enlist and encourage support from your organization is instrumental in your success. People will be inspired to work with you as they witness the commitment you have made towards your own success. They would prefer to work with someone whose achievements shine a bright light on their contributions rather than those who are just trying to get by.

IF YOU ARE LOOKING FOR A NAME FOR YOUR BUSINESS TRY ME INCORPORATED.

Running your own business inside your employer's framework is both possible and desirable. The beauty of it is that instead of creating your own products and services, finance, and human resources departments, you can take advantage of the structures already in place. You don't have to think about marketing, delivery or making payroll each week. You have a salary and a pay plan that allows you the freedom to focus on your goals. Given these advantages, you can spend your energies, talents, and abilities to make Me Incorporated as successful as possible.

There is an old saying, "Once you get a job you should look for work." Doing just what is required isn't good enough if you want to advance and make the most of your opportunities. Going above and beyond is the way to maximize your pay plan and put you in line for advancement. Looking for work at your job means finding ways to make yourself more valuable. Participate in company feedback sessions by sharing good ideas, volunteer to join internal marketing strategy committees, and suggest product enhancements or improvements. Share customer feedback with management or help colleagues through your knowledge and experience. As CEO of your own business, your input and support for improving your employer's business has the direct effect of improving the possibilities for your personal success.

Increasing sales and crushing quota is the result of how well you run your business and the best way to measure your effectiveness as CEO of Me Incorporated. It is not enough to only do what managers ask of you.

Their goals and requirements are going to be too low. Think of these goals as a good starting point and then put on your own CEO hat to envision what you want to achieve. Take time to plan what it will take to realize your vision and then get started. Success is achieved by working each day towards your goals through activities that are focused and aligned with your vision and plan.

Being the CEO of your own business inside the framework of your employer's company is also a state of mind. It is taking personal responsibility for your success or failure. When you do this, your prospects and customers will respond well and your colleagues will support your efforts. Let everyone see you lead by example and continually demonstrate a commitment to creating success. As you earn more money and increase the enjoyment of your job, management will see you in a new and better light.

Chapter 16 - Leverage Your Contacts

There are two types of prospects, those you know, and those you don't know yet. And the biggest problem for sellers is how to meet the ones you don't know. This is especially true if you haven't the luxury of a proactive marketing organization that drives inbound leads to the sales team. For most, this will be the case.

It is much easier to set up sales calls if you are fortunate enough to have a wide network of acquaintances and current or previous customers, people who will most likely take your call or answer your emails. They either already know you or have some connection with a mutual contact, event or organization. These are the individuals you should always leverage first when prospecting for new business. You will want to incorporate information on how you know each other or are mutually connected as part of your initial phone call or email. This may not ultimately win business. However, it may get you access and an opportunity to talk about the value you represent. Here is a good example from my own experience of what salespeople are faced with when trying to reach prospects and why even a thread of relationship can help:

Years ago, I was asked by my manager to contact a previous customer. My manager had prior dealings with this vice-president, and I was told to reference his name when I called to schedule a meeting. The vice-president picked up his phone on my first try. I explained who I was, referenced my manager, and asked for an appointment. I was told to call back in a few days and he would be glad to set up a time to meet with me. I did as I was told, but was unsuccessful in connecting with him. I continued to reach out by phone and email for over six months even though there was no response. Finally, I decided to give him one last call. To my surprise, he picked up the phone. Since he was very familiar with who I was, given all of the follow-up messages I had left, he agreed to meet with me.

As we settled down to talk during our meeting, he thanked me for my persistence and motioned to his desk where there were two telephones. He explained that one phone was the number he gave out to the general public, including salespeople. It was the phone he never answered. The other phone line was for people he wanted to reach him. It had been a mistake when he picked up the salesperson phone to answer my call.

> *EVEN THOUGH A NEW CONTACT MAY HAVE LITTLE OR NOTHING TO DO WITH YOUR PRODUCT OR SERVICE, THEY MAY BE A CONTACT NOW OR IN THE FUTURE THAT YOU CAN LEVERAGE.*

In today's highly competitive business environment, buyers are deluged by salespeople eager to have a conversation about their products and services. It can be so overwhelming. Many buyers simply don't answer their phone calls unless the caller ID shows someone with whom they have a connection. Lead generation services often provide salespeople with a prospect's direct dial, cell phone number, and email address. This means that a buyer may receive solicitations through any and all of these channels. There's no place to hide except by ignoring all contacts other than the ones coming from an existing relationship that they choose to acknowledge.

A good strategy to leverage your previous contacts is to put the name of a mutual acquaintance, organization, or place where you have met in the subject line of a pre-approach email. A pre-approach email is used to warm up your initial call to a prospect. The email works to leverage your connection to the prospect and introduce your name and company so that you are not entirely unknown when placing a follow-up phone call. It also gives you a psychological boost in that you are not making a totally cold call, rather one where the prospect may already know who you are and your mutual connection. Whether the prospect has even read your email is of no consequence. It gives you a more comfortable starting point for the conversation and a potential hook with which to engage the person on the other end of the line.

Leveraging your relationships is the most effective way to prospect. Always first use those that you have, and then find the ways that work best to meet new people with whom you can build a relationship. Try these methods:

- **Join a professional organization and get involved with a committee**
- **Work a trade show in reverse by attending and introducing yourself to attendees and people staffing the exhibit booths**
- **Use your value statement with people you meet at social events, PTO meetings, conventions, or on the golf course**
- **Swap your business card with people in complementary businesses**
- **Participate in a business to business networking group**
- **Attend user group meetings of the products or services you sell**

The idea is that people know people. Even though a new contact may have little or nothing to do with your product or service, they may be a contact now or in the future that you can leverage. Be sure to carry your business card and always ask to swap cards if appropriate. And for your records, write how and where you met on the back. It's a small world especially inside of certain industries and professions. And you never know how a contact, no matter how brief, may be leveraged.

Organizations will sometimes use lead generation services that promise to set up phone calls with decision makers. These services are typically very expensive while the return on investment is very low to non-existent. You will come to understand that no other person or organization can adequately express and convey the value of your products and services as well as you can.

If you are fortunate to have lead generation professionals in your company, their job is to identify and pass leads to their sales team partners. These leads may come from both the company's inbound or organic outbound marketing efforts. Companies often use popular lead generation and nurturing platforms, social media, and other online tools to induce prospects to request information or a demo. Lead generation professionals are trained to use their skills and expertise to promptly follow up on these requests, qualify them, and hand them off to the sales team at the right time in the sales process. You may even have the opportunity to coach these professionals on how to successfully produce results.

Whether you are handed qualified leads or you are on your own to generate prospects, the key is to turn people you don't know into people with whom you have a relationship. This can be a multi-step process or it can be relatively quick. It all hinges on the urgency of the prospect's needs, decision process and timeline, and your ability to rapidly build rapport. Often, you will need to have multiple touch points with a prospect over weeks or months. This is influenced by the complexity and cost of what you sell coupled with the internal buying process of your prospect's organization. Regardless, building a trusted and responsive relationship with your prospect will be key to ultimately closing a sale.

Chapter 17 – Make Cold Calling More Effective

Suppose you are hired as a Business Development Manager for a mid-size IT consulting company and work in its local branch office. It's a great company that offers a wide range of valuable and very sellable professional and consulting services. On the first day, you are assigned a desk, given a computer, an email address, a telephone, and access to the company's internal systems. Your manager says that the territory is wide open and you can prospect whomever you want. Then you are left alone to figure out how to get started.

FOR MANY SALESPEOPLE, THE MOST UNCOMFORTABLE PART OF CALLING COLD PROSPECTS IS NOT KNOWING WHAT TO SAY WHEN SOMEONE ANSWERS.

Your employer uses a sales model that pairs technical resources with a salesperson to assist in the sales process. This is a great help, since you need to learn about the products and services you are selling. Listening to a sales engineer's presentation to prospective customers is an education. What the technical partner cannot do is set up these meetings. That is your job. You quickly learn that you will have to develop sales leads as your company won't be providing them. Cold calling will be the primary way to prospect.

For many salespeople, the most uncomfortable part of calling cold prospects is not knowing what to say when someone answers. Your message needs to be something that will be immediately engaging. It's hard enough to get prospects on the phone; don't waste any opportunities to make a connection and ask for a meeting. Use a script that gives you a starting point and direction for the conversation. If you have to make it up on the spot, you may stutter or stammer, and even want to hang up when your call is answered.

You want your script to quickly differentiate you and your company from the overwhelming number of cold calls your prospects receive almost daily. Because of this deluge, your approach will need to be respectful and sensitive to the interruption caused by your call. Here are a few guidelines to incorporate in a script:

- **Identify yourself by name and the company you represent**
- **Acknowledge the interruption and ask for a moment of the prospect's time**
- **Share your geographical location and the potential value you can provide**
- **End with an open-ended statement, not a yes or no question**

Try writing a script something like this, "Good morning Sue, this is Bill Moody calling from Hi-Tech Partners in Newton. I'm sure I'm interrupting something… do you have a moment to speak with me? I work with life sciences companies in the greater Boston area to assure that they meet FDA cybersecurity guidelines for new medical device submissions. Given your company's product line, I thought our testing might be of interest to you."

This type of script is effective in helping overcome the discomfort of starting a cold conversation. At first, you may want to read it verbatim which can feel stiff and unnatural. Over time the words will become second nature and you will be able to modify the script based on who you are calling and the products or services in your portfolio that you want to emphasize. You may even start to feel comfortable enough to add some gentle humor if it feels right, such as, "I'm sure you get a million of these calls!" Prospects will respond well to this approach for a few reasons:

First, you clearly identify yourself and the company you represent because a prospect may have heard of your company and have a favorable impression of it.

Second, you didn't assume that the prospect had time to talk at that moment, rather you asked for permission to continue the conversation.

Third, they heard that your company was local, and prospects tend to like doing business with a local company. If your company does business across the U.S. or in a particular geographic area that is relevant to your prospect, you can point that out to the same effect.

Fourth, you shared the services your company represents in a way that projects potential value and demonstrates domain knowledge through an understanding of a specific requirement highly relevant to the prospect's industry.

Fifth, the script ended with a statement and not a question. The statement was designed to draw out a response, not simply a yes or no answer to further the conversation.

Remember that it's hard to get prospects on the phone and you want to be as prepared as possible to engage with them. Cold calling can be effective even though it tends to be a low return method of prospecting. There are ways to make it more productive, including the use of a pre-approach email or voicemail that can warm up a prospect and prepare them for your call. For starters, try writing your own script to see the difference it can make in your cold-calling results.

Chapter 18 – To Develop Big Deals, Start Small

Experience has shown that getting an opportunity to compete for a big deal, other than through an RFP, requires a customer to believe that your company has the capacity and proven capability to successfully deliver large projects. Big projects expose the decision maker to risking their company's resources and operational efficiency should the engagement end badly. Even more importantly, the decision maker may also face the potential of diminishing their reputation or losing their job if the project fails. The decision maker needs confidence to include your company in their list of competing vendors. This confidence is generated by proving your company's value through delivering successful small engagements.

As a way to begin a working relationship with a new prospect, a proven strategy is to ask if you can be given an opportunity to deliver a relatively small or low-risk project. A small project gives the customer, at low risk, an opportunity to assess how your delivery people work with the customer's team, the quality of their work, and adherence to the agreed upon timeline and budget. Effectively completing a small project is the most direct way to build a successful relationship and give you access to more critical, strategic, and bigger initiatives.

> *BIG DEALS TEND TO BE LOW PROBABILITY WINS.*
> *TO DEVELOP BIG DEALS, START SMALL.*

If you are fortunate enough to earn an invitation to compete for a major project, here are some things to keep in mind:

- **Evaluate the opportunity with your sales leadership**
- **Determine if there is a reasonable chance your company can win the engagement**
- **Consider if your company can demonstrate previous successes delivering projects of a similar size using the required skills and expertise**
- **Discuss the potential competitors and the vendors already entrenched at your customer and the relationships they may already have in place**
- **Determine if the project will be profitable and if it makes good business sense to commit the time, energy, and resources that may distract from more winnable opportunities**

Big deals tend to be low probability wins. If you win a big one, great. If you lose it and haven't taken the time to develop a range of higher probability wins, you end up with little or nothing to show for all of your hard work. To develop big deals, start small.

There is an understandable tendency on the part of new and sometimes veteran salespeople to go after big deals and ignore smaller opportunities. Big deals offer enticing rewards including large commission checks, the envy of peers, kudos from management, and the benefit of retiring a significant chunk of quota. But big deals require a huge investment of time and energy and have a lower probability of closing than smaller deals. Remember that the opportunity to participate in big deals often comes by winning smaller deals.

It is a winning philosophy to work on deals of any size that have a good probability of closing. You will have your share of big sales and they will be fun and profitable. Filling your pipeline with quality opportunities of different sizes will give you the best results for consistently closing business and the most return on your time and efforts. Your job is to throw lots of good opportunities into a pot. The more you put in, the better the likelihood is of something good boiling up. You can work your business in this manner unless your mandate is to only work on large opportunities.

It's better to be consistent in closing business than it is to lose a big deal and have nothing because you have ignored smaller opportunities while pursuing the big score. Take a look at your pipeline. If you don't have potential deals that span a range of sizes, think again about how you are approaching your business. This is especially true if you are new to sales or just starting a new sales job. Build your book of business by taking every opportunity that you personally generate or comes your way, and doing your best to close it. Small deals are often the gateway to larger opportunities. Here is another example of a big lesson that I learned early in my career:

While working in a retail setting selling electronics at a well-known national chain store, I was paid an hourly wage along with a commission earned on my sales each week. I quickly recognized that more money could be made by selling the high-priced audio equipment, police scanners, radios, and other devices, rather than the electronic parts, batteries, TV antennae equipment, and the myriad of other small items in the store. Since there were always other salespeople working with me who were competing for business, it often became a race to engage a customer who showed interest in the more expensive things we sold. The reality was that we ended up spending lots of time with these prospective high spending buyers only to be disappointed when they didn't make a purchase.

There was an older salesman in the store that didn't try to compete in the same manner and consistently earned the highest weekly commission. He simply took each customer as they came up to the counter to pay for items they had selected. He wrote up sales whether they were big, small, or medium-sized. There were opportunities for him to show and sell the big-ticket items as well, however, by not focusing on those, he used his time more efficiently and profitably.

He demonstrated that to be a consistently high earner, the focus should be on closing each piece of business regardless of its size. Think about similar guidelines given what you sell. Your ultimate success will be measured by how steadily you bring in quality business that fits the profile of a good prospect for your company's products and services. You'll still have opportunities to make big sales when they come along and your pipeline will reflect a healthy, mix of business.

Chapter 19 - Prepare for Success

It is well known that a person's ability to recognize opportunities and then act on them is essential for success in life. The same is true in sales. Your ability to see where your products and services can have a beneficial impact on prospects and customers, and your ability to engage in meaningful interactions to prove that impact, are key to your success. Preparedness is the other essential ingredient. Where opportunity meets preparation is where you want to be.

Preparation is mandatory in almost all endeavors. Luck may sometimes play a part, but luck can't be counted on. What some people define as luck are actually logical outcomes when you become knowledgeable, experienced, and focused in pursuit of your goals. In sales, the more you develop information about your products, services, sales skills, and strategies, the luckier you will become. Become a student of your industry. It is important to understand, albeit sometimes at an advanced level, the terms and technical jargon that is commonly used by customers and technical colleagues. Be prepared for sales interactions by becoming conversant with current and new trends in your industry so that you will be aware and ready for these potential discussion points.

BECOME A STUDENT OF YOUR INDUSTRY.

Preparation is also crucial to conduct quality and effective sales interactions. If you are selling in a team environment, be sure to hold a pre-meeting prep session. You want to ensure that your team has a unified approach to the meeting, a clear understanding of roles and responsibilities, and approval of any visual aids that may be used. If possible, send a draft agenda to your customer and ask for feedback to make sure that what you are planning meets their expectations. Prepare for meetings that you conduct on your own in the same manner. In either case, be sure to have a clear understanding of what you want to accomplish. This will help keep meetings on track and focused. You never want to wing it when you interact with a customer. Meetings are too hard to come by to waste.

Think about which aspects of your product knowledge, sales skills, the market you serve, and your ability to hold productive calls and meetings, need strengthening. There are many resources you can use to improve in these areas. Your close rate, income, and career advancement will improve when you are prepared for every sales situation that comes your way.

Chapter 20 – Guide Your Prospects

One of the most effective roles a salesperson performs is to guide prospects and customers through the maze of purchasing choices available to them. To be an effective guide, it's necessary to have a solid understanding of what your products and services are designed to do and your prospect's reasons for making a purchase. It will also be very helpful if you have information on competing products and services. Most of your employers will develop talking points about competitors that can be very useful. Without product knowledge, even the best qualifying skills won't enable you to guide your prospect to a potential solution to their problem. Worse, you may miss significant opportunities to suggest creative ways in which your products and services may come into play, and possibly increase the size of the sale and add value to your business relationship.

Guidance is also one of the building blocks of lasting sales success. Regardless of what you sell, your advice can save valuable time in a buyer's decision process. It can also inform them of options about which they know little or nothing. When you find you're in a new sales position and don't have a good grasp of what you are selling or even the full scope of what you can offer, it can be very uncomfortable. You will need to quickly learn about your products and services so that you know enough to start prospecting. Experience shows that it takes around six months to become conversant with a line of new of things to sell. The important thing is to learn every day through study, asking questions of colleagues, and the experience of doing your job.

> ***REGARDLESS OF WHAT YOU SELL, YOUR ADVICE CAN SAVE VALUABLE TIME IN A BUYER'S DECISION PROCESS.***

Customers won't always recognize your guidance as relevant or meaningful. It may be perceived as self-serving or simply misinterpreted. In these situations, if you feel strongly that your advice is particularly valuable, attempt to make yourself heard. Sometimes your customer won't be able to see the forest for the trees. Your guidance and advice, if given in the right spirit and with confidence, can make all the difference. Learning to be a good guide is more than product knowledge and persistence. It's helping a prospect recognize the value you are offering. Develop the soft skills of patience and active listening, along with clear verbal and writing skills. These abilities can often turn a negative decision into a positive one.

Chapter 21 - Become an Effective Facilitator

There is a common misperception about what it takes for a salesperson to close business. Most successful salespeople know that you are not able to sell anything to anyone until a prospect is ready to become a buyer. Non-sellers and salespeople that are early in their careers often don't understand how this works, and they think:

If I don't sell my products or services, how will I make my quota or keep my job?

If I'm not supposed to sell, then what is the point of the sales training I have been given?

These are great questions and the answer is simple. To become a successful salesperson, first become an effective facilitator. Merriam-Webster defines a facilitator as, "someone who helps to bring about an outcome.... by providing indirect or unobtrusive assistance, guidance, or supervision." The keywords here are unobtrusive, assistance, and guidance.

If you sell technical products and services, realize that your prospects don't want to talk technical requirements with you. What they want is a separate conversation with your technical colleagues with whom they can discuss in depth the technical problems they are trying to solve. They will appreciate your ability to smoothly set up appropriate conversations, ensure the right technical team will be present, and run a well-prepared and thoughtful meeting. Further, your prospects will see the value you provide in being the single point of contact to move them through the process of proposal, approval, final paperwork, and start date. Your role is to facilitate the sales process and make it as smooth, efficient, and effective as possible for your prospects and company.

> *YOU ARE IN THE BEST POSITION TO ORGANIZE AND COORDINATE THE SALES PURSUIT IN AN EFFICIENT MANNER.*

Whether you are a professional selling highly technical, or less complex products and services, your effective facilitation of sales calls, presentations, and demos is key to successfully closing business. This is especially true if you involve a team of people from your company. Establish right away that there can be only one leader in your group, and you are that person. You are in the best position to organize and coordinate the sales pursuit in an efficient manner.

Strong facilitation starts with adequate preparation for your team, whether it is made up of many individuals or just you and a single technical resource. It is your job to schedule a pre-appointment prep call to present and discuss the information you have gathered on the prospect and their needs. During this conversation, roles should be assigned and your leadership confirmed for the upcoming meeting. The customer's technical issues and your team's potential approach need to be discussed and agreed upon. Any supporting technical materials and documentation that will be used should be assigned to the appropriate resource to prepare. For complex technical discussions with the client, a final prep meeting should be scheduled. Adequate preparation will allow you to keep sales calls on-track and focused on the original intent and goals for the meeting.

> *ALL THE BEST SALES TRAINING AVAILABLE WON'T YIELD A SALE WITHOUT THE RIGHT FACILITATION.*

During the meeting with your prospect think of yourself as the master of ceremonies:

- **Confirm the time allotted**
- **Ask for introductions**
- **Recap the premise for why you have gotten together**
- **Direct specific questions to your team members**
- **Gain agreement on next steps**
- **Close the meeting**

After everyone has been introduced, be sure to ask whether anything has changed since you first scheduled the meeting. This is a tremendously important question. If you fail to ask this critical question you may find your meeting to be of no value, especially if you start talking about an approach that is no longer of importance. Circumstances often change between setting up a meeting and sitting down with a prospect or customer. Your preparation and approach may no longer be relevant and it is up to you as the facilitator to guide the discussion in a new and more meaningful direction. Sometimes the discussion may go off on a tangent that has little relevance to the key concerns expressed by the prospect. Your strong facilitation and guidance will be needed to bring the conversation back on track. It is up to you to make sure the discussion goes in the right direction and achieves predetermined goals.

Sales training is important. However, all the best sales training available won't yield a sale without the right facilitation. A professional salesperson provides unobtrusive assistance, guidance, and supervision during the sales process and enjoys building relationships based on these qualities. Prospects and customers will appreciate your approach and selling will become less stressful and more enjoyable. Learn to be an effective facilitator and you will greatly improve your close rate.

Chapter 22 - Don't Leave Money on the Table

Many salespeople have a sales plan that includes a base salary, and a bonus or commission based on a percentage of either gross or net sales. Gross sales are the total dollars of a sales transaction minus things like shipping and taxes. Net sales are based on the margin, or gross profit, built into the selling price of the goods and services sold. Some salespeople receive a bonus instead of a commission. This can be based on the salesperson's individual performance, the overall performance of the team of which they are a member, or the company as a whole. Sometimes a sales plan will include accelerators. These are incentives to reward exceptional performance and can be very meaningful to a salesperson's total compensation. There are as many variations on sales plans as there are sales organizations. You will experience numerous plans when you make selling your career.

> **ASK FOR AS MUCH DETAILED INFORMATION AS POSSIBLE ABOUT THE COMPENSATION PLAN BEFORE YOU ACCEPT THE POSITION.**

There is a saying in the world of financial investing that no one ever went broke taking a profit. The same can be said for the different compensation models under which you will work. Some plans are simply better and more lucrative than others. All, however, will reward you for producing positive results. It will be up to you to decide whether the plan, and consequently the job and company for whom you work, is a good fit. Most salespeople will work for a number of employers throughout their careers. If you become a consistent producer there will be opportunities to move up to better and more lucrative positions. If you don't, there is an adage in the form of a riddle: What do you call a salesperson who doesn't sell? Unemployed.

When interviewing for a new sales job, ask for as much detailed information as possible about the compensation plan before you accept the position. You won't always get it, but it's essential that you have at least a broad understanding of how it works. It should always be in writing, and the easier to understand the better. If it is long, complicated, and hard for your new manager to explain, be careful. You will work hard at your new position and it is important to feel that you will be adequately rewarded. Try to get the questions you have answered before you say yes to an offer:

Will your plan include extra money to help soften the first months of your new job with a draw?
Does the At Plan compensation package for your position seem achievable?

There are two types of draws. The first is a draw against future commissions. This means that you will receive a guaranteed amount of money in addition to your salary for a specific number of months as you ramp up to closing business. The money paid as a draw is owed to your employer and future commissions will be used to repay the draw. The second type of draw is considered non-recoverable. The money advanced under this type of draw is given without any expectations that you will repay it from future commissions. The difference between the two types is similar to either receiving financial aid for college in the form of a loan or as a scholarship grant. Go for non-recoverable whenever possible.

A RULE OF THUMB IS THAT DOING YOUR JOB SHOULD NEVER COST YOU MONEY.

Try to get a good feel for the quota you will be assigned. This is the best way to determine if the At Plan compensation is a realistic number. You can ask how many of the current salespeople were able to achieve quota in the last year. This will give you a sense of your ability as a salesperson new to the organization to come up to speed quickly. It's better to start a new sales job with a realistic picture of what can be achieved. At Plan earnings are a target set up by your employer, however, they may not always represent what is possible.

Compensation packages vary greatly. Aside from a salary or hourly pay rate they may include:

- **Commissions or bonuses**
- **Stock grants**
- **Employer contributions to a 401K or other retirement plans**
- **Paid time off**
- **Health insurance**
- **Holiday and sick pay**

Your package may also cover reimbursable expenses such as client entertainment, car, and company travel. A rule of thumb is that doing your job should never cost you money. Your employer is obligated to support the client work you do on the company's behalf. You are entitled to be repaid for anything you pay for out of pocket if it is in pursuit of company business.

Some plans will also offer a skills improvement budget that can be used for sales training, attendance at conferences, and other product-related education. If such a budget is offered, take advantage of it. You never know how much it will improve your performance or come into play when applying to a new job. The more effective you make yourself through education, the more valuable will be the opportunities and attendant compensations as you advance through your career.

Chapter 23 – Maximize Your Compensation Plan

When a new compensation plan is introduced it can bring opportunities for some salespeople to make more money. For others, it can mean challenges to adjust their book of business to reflect the realities of how they will be paid going forward. Regardless of what a comp plan includes, understand that it is always your job as a salesperson to maximize your earnings. This means earning the highest amount your comp plan offers through base salary, commission, bonus and any other incentives that may be offered. When you maximize your earnings, you will realize your financial goals and support opportunities to advance in your career.

> ***REGARDLESS OF HOW A PLAN IS STRUCTURED, A STRATEGY IS NEEDED TO ACHIEVE THE RESULTS YOU WANT.***

While changes to your comp plan may seem arbitrary and random at first glance, it is important to remember that comp plans are set up to encourage and reward certain behaviors and results. Some plans emphasize acquiring new accounts, selling high-margin products and services, or expanding business within existing accounts. Often accelerators or special incentives are placed on selling a new offering or when you exceed quota. These can sweeten a comp plan and provide a path to substantially increased earnings. Regardless of how a plan is structured, a strategy is needed to achieve the results you want.

The first step in creating a strategy is to know your plan inside and out. The more complex the plan, the more the need to analyze it in order to ensure that you know exactly how to comply with all of its nuanced requirements. Ask yourself these questions:

- **What is my quota and over what time period is it measured?**
- **Are there details in the plan regarding close dates, specific gross, or net margin goals?**
- **What is the definition of a net-new account?**
- **How is account ownership determined?**
- **What is the time period for incentives to sell certain items or services?**
- **What risks do you run to your overall book of business and existing accounts by putting most of your focus on incentives?**
- **How do all of these factors affect your compensation?**

Once you answer all of these questions, you're ready to put a selling strategy in place. Be sure to consider where your biggest financial return lies as you create your strategy. This can sometimes be from selling specific products or services or acquiring new customers.

To create an effective strategy, start with your end goals in mind. Review your assigned quota, gross or net margin, new account acquisition, and other specific targets. Analyze your current book of business to estimate how each customer will contribute to your targets. Then create a list of prospects that can utilize what you sell and the financial ability to buy your products and services. Determine how these prospects will potentially contribute to realizing your goals.

TO CREATE AN EFFECTIVE STRATEGY, START WITH YOUR END GOALS IN MIND.

Now think about the special incentives in your sales plan. Look at your existing customers to see which of them may present good possibilities to help you take advantage of these motivators, or whether it will be necessary to close deals with new accounts. Be sure to put all of these projections and numbers down on paper or use a spreadsheet program. Organizing your strategy makes it easy to change numbers when mapping what-if scenarios.

Once you have decided on your approach, focus on the input, not the outcome. Your level of focused activities, your strong work ethic, and drive are what will make a successful strategy a reality. As the year progresses, remember to review your strategy often to make changes and modifications as needed. Your comp plan's total earnings At Plan is a great guide to what you can accomplish, however it is only a guide. Reality can be vastly different. Your monthly or quarterly commission check will be a reflection of how effectively you are succeeding. Be sure to review your commission statements with a very careful eye as to their accuracy and math. Don't be afraid to fight for what you believe is your due. It isn't enough to assume that the manager or financial analyst who calculates your commission or bonus has all of the information or understanding of your plan to get every payment correct.

By taking time to create as clear a strategy as possible, you will have the best opportunity to maximize your earnings whenever there is a change to your comp plan. It is an exercise that will pay big dividends in more money, career advancement, and your ability to focus on productive sales activities. Remember, the more money you earn, the better your company succeeds and the more fun you have.

Chapter 24 - Put It All Together

Proven sales concepts and strategies can create strong relationships, robust pipelines, and lots of closed sales. Being successful requires that you learn more than just the rudiments of how the sales process works. It includes your development of meaningful interpersonal and communication skills, and the experience that can only be gained by being actively engaged in sales activities. If you are new to selling or have been selling for years, there will always be ways to up your game, improve your win rate and, adjust your techniques to bring greater success. There is no way to rush this process. You must stay focused on bringing your best effort to your work every day and allow successes to accumulate over time.

Jackie Chan, the world-famous martial arts expert and movie star, said that he started working on his Kung Fu skills at age seven and spent the next ten years under the strict tutelage of his master instructor. He then went on to spend another eight years making countless Kung Fu films as an actor and fight director, all of them flops. Broke and discouraged, he took a job as a waiter in a Chinese restaurant. His big break came when he landed a role with a movie producer who asked Jackie what type of martial arts film he would like to make. No one had ever asked Jackie this before and he had been stuck making films in which the director had tried to have him emulate the famous Bruce Lee. Copying Bruce Lee's unique style was impossible and stifled Jackie's development of his own distinctive style. The producer allowed Jackie to use his creativity and personality in his roles. This freed him to develop the exciting, fun-filled, and comedic style that has made him a household name. It only took Jackie fifteen years of effort to become an overnight success. Even when things went poorly, Jackie never lost sight of his end goal of becoming a movie star. His dedication, training, and persistence enabled him to reach his goal.

> *IF YOU ARE NEW TO SELLING OR HAVE BEEN SELLING FOR YEARS, THERE WILL ALWAYS BE WAYS TO UP YOUR GAME, IMPROVE YOUR WIN RATE AND, ADJUST YOUR TECHNIQUES TO BRING GREATER SUCCESS.*

Your journey to a successful sales career should be much quicker than Jackie's. Selling, just like any worthy profession, takes time, effort, and perseverance to master. You will have successes and flops along the way. It's important to stay focused on your goals, work each day to improve and learn, develop your own style of selling, and enjoy the journey. Consistent, persistent, and focused effort on the right activities is what creates success.

It can be easy to get lost in what are referred to as no-pay activities. These are actions that many salespeople use to fool themselves into thinking that they are selling when they are only keeping busy. Some examples of no-pay activities are: talking with colleagues, shuffling papers, making plans without taking action, and keeping busy doing unproductive tasks. No-pay activities don't require direct contact with a prospect or customer. They don't require you to ask difficult or uncomfortable questions. They don't expose you to rejection or disappointment. No-pay activities also end in poor sales performance, job insecurity, and unpleasant conversations with your manager. They are called no-pay activities because they result in either no commissions or worse, the loss of your position.

Pay activities involve prospecting, setting appointments, and holding meetings with qualified prospects. They also include writing proposals, negotiating deals, finalizing paperwork for purchases, and setting delivery, and project start dates. Stay focused on pay activities. They are where the rewards are. Pay activities are what make selling a productive, lucrative, and exciting career.

Chapter 25 – Focus on the Input, Not the Outcome

A common problem in sales is the end-game pressure to produce results, achieve quota, or drive margin. While these measures are key for a successful salesperson, too much focus on the wrong end of the sales cycle can create stress, frustration, and paralysis.

Selling is a process. There is no way around that fact. Sometimes the process is short, however, the process is often long and has many twists and turns. The last step, the close, can seem almost anti-climactic after all of the work that has gone into getting to that point. It is the close that sellers see as the most important. After all, if you don't close a deal, how will you earn a commission? The problem is that too much energy can be put into the destination instead of the journey. It is the journey through the sales cycle, which includes the process and input of sales activities, that gets you to the destination. Without the right activities or input, the desired outcome may never happen.

A salesperson's job is to throw lots of potential sales opportunities into a large pot. Keep this image in mind as you experience the ups and downs of building and pursuing your pipeline. Don't worry about the size of the deal, the potential commission, or the immediate impact on your quota. Just maintain the image of tossing more and more opportunities into your pot to keep things boiling. Focus on the day to day activities needed. This input keeps you from getting sidetracked by only focusing on results. You will notice that if you consistently do the right things, you will get the outcomes you want, whether these are large commission checks or regular praise from your sales leadership.

WITHOUT THE RIGHT ACTIVITIES OR INPUT, THE DESIRED OUTCOME MAY NEVER HAPPEN.

Of course, the outcome is important. Always decide on the result that you want whether that relates to your quota or some other metric. By focusing on the outcome and not the process, you can create frustration and unwanted pressure. Positive end results are only possible by doing what's necessary to move through the sales cycle. Continual input frees up the mind to bring the creativity, energy, and urgency needed to your daily activities. Stay focused on the input and let go of the outcome and you will find your work more rewarding and successful.

Chapter 26 – Enjoy the Journey

Selling is a craft, and like all crafts, it takes training and experience to perfect. The basics can be learned easily, however, the most valuable lessons are learned during actual engagement in the full scope of the sales cycle.

Thorough and thoughtful sales methodologies will only take you so far. The mechanics of sales are important. Sales mechanics and processes need to be infused with strong communication skills, empathy, rapport building, and common sense. The old saying: "People don't care how much you know until they know how much you care," is a key concept in successful selling. It is often these soft sales skills that turn a would-be buyer and prospect into a customer. A salesperson can follow all of the steps of a given sales process, check all the boxes, and say all the right words. Without meaningful interpersonal skills, they won't succeed to their highest effect.

We have become a people highly cynical about others' motives. The concept of trust, so valuable in any interpersonal relationship, takes a particularly hard hit as relates to sales. Long-lasting business relationships have no chance of existing without trust. A buyer must believe in the integrity of a seller's commitment to provide the products and services as advertised. Keeping one's word can only be proven by actions. These actions are the building blocks of trust. In a world where so much can be artifice and insincerity, trust is hard to come by. If a buyer finds they can trust their salesperson, good things will happen at that time and potentially over an extended period.

BRING YOUR BEST EFFORTS EVERY DAY AND STAY FOCUSED ON YOUR GOALS.

Tom Hank's character in the movie A League of Their Own said, "Baseball is supposed to be hard. If it wasn't hard, everyone would do it. The hard is what makes it great." The same can be said of top-tier salespeople. The talent, hard work, perseverance, and commitment it takes to make it to the major leagues of baseball, are the same qualities that build great salespeople. While many major league ballplayers are not elite all-stars, they have still reached a highly successful level in their profession. Strive to achieve the level of success that you decide is right for you. Bring your best efforts every day and stay focused on your goals. Remember that success isn't a place you arrive, rather it is a compounding of daily achievements along the journey of your career.

Make sure you give a lot of thought to what success means to you. Without knowing where you want to go you usually end up someplace else. Sales can bring you financial rewards beyond anything you might imagine. It can build your self-esteem, bring the admiration of your peers, and create friendships and long business relationships with customers, colleagues, and suppliers. Sales can open up new horizons and worlds including travel and increased responsibilities. It can provide fun and satisfaction through accomplishments and achievements you never thought possible.

A career in sales also comes with its own risks and challenges. Most salespeople will work for a number of organizations over the course of their careers. Moving from one company to another can happen for many different reasons, some are within your control and some are not. Circumstances outside of your control can include a bad fit with a direct manager, employer downsizing, relocating or going out of business, recession, or a host of other reasons that may or may not make sense to you. It can be shocking to lose a position. One moment you have a comfortable income and a good career trajectory. The next thing you know, you may be on unemployment compensation and trying to figure out where to go from there.

Remember, the circumstances that you can control during your sales career are your work ethic, willingness to learn, reliability, treatment of co-workers, adherence to company policies, honesty, and customer relations. The good news is that if you have developed solid sales skills, created a positive track record, and haven't burnt bridges with former colleagues, there will always be another sales position you can acquire. Good salespeople, regardless of how experienced, are always needed. Recognize that most sales positions have a limited shelf life. Do as well as you can, for as long as you can wherever you are, and you will have little trouble finding your next job. Create, represent, and deliver value, infused with your personality and approach, be trustworthy, and have fun. Enjoy the sales journey and the rewards that a successful selling career provides.

Dave is an accomplished author, coach, sales manager, and quota-busting salesman. He is the recipient of multiple sales and sales management awards, and the author of *The Sales Value Chain: A Guide to Creating Value for Your Customers & Your Career*. His LinkedIn publications include many insightful articles on sales and selling concepts. He is also the creator of *The Fundamentals of Humanistic Selling Workshop* and other online training series.

The majority of Dave's career has been in the information technology consulting and professional services business. Dave has held positions as an Industry Vice-President, Director of Sales, Business Development Manager, Account Executive, and Territory Manager. His career has included working for companies such as marchFirst, Whitman-Hart, International Network Services, TUV Rheinland, OpenSky Corporation, and Kelly IT Resources.

Dave's insights are based on strategies and principals proven to produce outstanding results and career-long customers. He is committed to helping salespeople achieve their business goals and maximize their potential. Dave believes the power of integrity, honesty, and respect builds strong business relationships and sales success.

For information about virtual coaching and speaking engagements contact dave@salesmentor.net or visit his website **www.salesmentor.net.**

www.ingramcontent.com/pod-product-compliance
Lightning Source LLC
Chambersburg PA
CBHW030445220526
45464CB00006B/2427